WOODROW WILSON

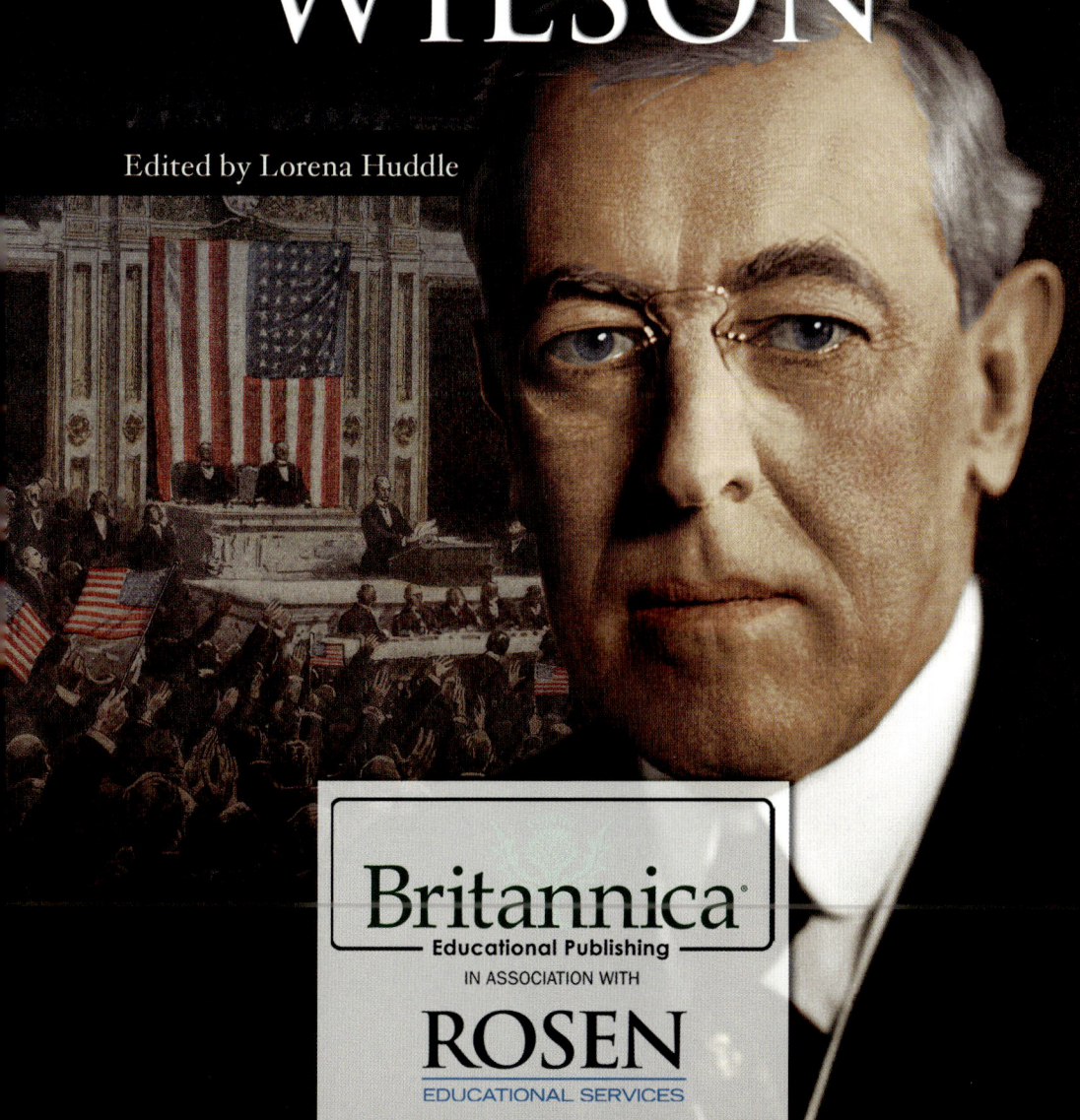

PIVOTAL PRESIDENTS
PROFILES IN LEADERSHIP

WOODROW WILSON

Edited by Lorena Huddle

Britannica
Educational Publishing

IN ASSOCIATION WITH

ROSEN
EDUCATIONAL SERVICES

Published in 2018 by Britannica Educational Publishing (a trademark of Encyclopædia Britannica, Inc.) in association with The Rosen Publishing Group, Inc.
29 East 21st Street, New York, NY 10010

Copyright © 2018 by Encyclopædia Britannica, Inc. Britannica, Encyclopædia Britannica, and the Thistle logo are registered trademarks of Encyclopædia Britannica, Inc. All rights reserved.

Rosen Publishing materials copyright © 2018 The Rosen Publishing Group, Inc. All rights reserved.

Distributed exclusively by Rosen Publishing.
To see additional Britannica Educational Publishing titles, go to rosenpublishing.com.

First Edition

Britannica Educational Publishing
J.E. Luebering: Executive Director, Core Editorial
Andrea R. Field: Managing Editor, Compton's by Britannica

Rosen Publishing
Kathy Kuhtz Campbell: Senior Editor
Nelson Sá: Art Director
Brian Garvey: Series Designer
Alison Hird: Book Layout
Cindy Reiman: Photography Manager
Bruce Donnola: Photo Researcher
Supplementary material by Lorena Huddle

Library of Congress Cataloging-in-Publication Data

Names: Huddle, Lorena, editor.
Title: Woodrow Wilson / editor, Lorena Huddle.
Description: New York: Britannica Educational Publishing, in Association with Rosen Educational Services, [2018] | Series: Pivotal Presidents: profiles in leadership | Includes bibliographical references and index. | Audience: Grades 7–12.
Identifiers: LCCN 2016053925 | ISBN 9781680486353 (library bound : alk. paper)
Subjects: LCSH: Wilson, Woodrow, 1856–1924—Juvenile literature. | Presidents—United States—Biography—Juvenile literature. | United States—Politics and government,—1913-1921—Juvenile literature.
Classification: LCC E767 .W875 2017 | DDC 973.91/3092 [B] —dc23
LC record available at https://lccn.loc.gov/2016053925

Manufactured in China

Photo credits: Cover, p. 3 (portrait) Stock Montage/Archive Photos/Getty Images; cover, p. 3 (background) Leemage/Universal Images Group/Getty Images; cover, pp. 1, 3 (flag) © iStockphoto.com/spxChrome; p. 6 ullstein bild/Getty Images; p. 13 Ian Dagnall/Alamy Stock Photo; pp. 14, 17, 38, 54, 60 Library of Congress Prints and Photographs Division; p. 18 Library of Congress, Washington, D.C. (cph 3c30978); p. 21 © Photos.com/Thinkstock; p. 23 PhotoQuest/Archive Photos/Getty Images; p. 25 Education Images/Universal Images Group/Getty Images; p. 29 Library of Congress/Corbis Historical/Getty Images; pp. 32, 55 Encyclopædia Britannica, Inc.; p. 33 Library of Congress, Washington, D.C. (cph 3a16546); p. 37 (top) Herbert Orth/The LIFE Picture Collection/Getty Images (detail); p. 37 (bottom) Robynrg/Shutterstock.com; p. 39 Center for Legislative Archives, National Archives, Washington, D.C.; p. 42 Time Life Pictures/The LIFE Picture Collection/Getty Images; pp. 45, 52 MPI/Archive Photos/Getty Images; p. 48 Americana/Encyclopædia Britannica, Inc.; p. 50 Library of Congress, Washington, D.C. (LC-USZC4-10297); p. 51 Library of Congress Manuscript Division; p. 58 De Agostini Picture Library/Getty Images; p. 63 Everett Historical/Shutterstock.com; p. 65 Andia/Universal Images Group/Getty Images; interior pages flag Fedorov Oleksiy/Shutterstock.com.

Table of Contents

Introduction 6

Chapter 1 Early Life and Education 11

Chapter 2 A Professor, University President, and Governor 20

Chapter 3 The Twenty-eighth President 31

Chapter 4 A Second Term and the Great War 47

Conclusion 64
Glossary 67
For More Information 70
For Further Reading 74
Index 77

INTRODUCTION

Woodrow Wilson, the twenty-eighth president of the United States, is best remembered for his legislative achievements and his leadership during World War I.

During World War I, in one of the most ambitious speeches in modern history, US President Woodrow Wilson attempted to rally the people of the world in a movement for a peace settlement that would remove the causes of future wars and establish an organization to maintain peace. In an address to the US Senate on January 22, 1917, he called for a "peace without victory" to be enforced by a league of nations that the United States would join and strongly support. He spoke again of this idea in his war message, adding that the United States wanted above all else to "make the world safe for democracy." When he failed to persuade the British and French leaders to join him in issuing a common statement of war aims, he went to Congress on January 8, 1918, to make, in his Fourteen Points address, his definitive declaration to the American people and the world.

In his general points Wilson demanded an end to the old diplomacy that had led to wars in the past. He proposed open diplomacy instead of entangling alliances, and he called for freedom of the seas, an impartial settlement of colonial claims, arms reduction, removal of artificial trade barriers, and, most important, a league of nations to promote peace and protect the territorial integrity and independence of its members. A breathtaking declaration, the Fourteen Points gave new hope to millions of liberals and moderate socialists who were fighting for a new international order based on peace and justice.

Determined to keep these points, Wilson made the controversial decision to go in person to the Paris Peace Conference, where he spent seven months in wearying, often angry negotiations with the British, French, and Italians. The final product, the Treaty of Versailles, was signed on June 28, 1919. Although the treaty fell short of Wilson's vision, it did provide for the creation of the League of Nations, which he believed would adjust international differences and maintain peace.

Wilson returned to the United States from the peace conference exhausted and in failing health. Republican senators sought either to reject the treaty or to attach reservations that would gravely limit America's commitments to the League of Nations. After two months of frustrating talks with senators, Wilson took his case to the people in September 1919 in the hope of shaping public opinion on this very important issue of the day. A master of the English language and public oratory, he threw himself into a whirlwind cross-country tour, giving thirty-nine speeches in three weeks.

The strain, both mental and physical, was too much for him. Wilson had a near breakdown on September 25, after which his doctor canceled the rest of the tour and rushed him back to Washington, DC. On October 2, 1910, Wilson suffered a massive stroke that left him partially paralyzed on his left side. His intellectual capacity was not affected, but his emotional balance and judgment were badly impaired. Although he gradually recovered from the worst effects of the stroke, Wilson never again fully functioned as president.

The peace treaty was defeated in the Senate. Wilson demanded that Democratic senators spurn all efforts at compromise with the Republicans. Twice the Treaty of Versailles failed to gain the two-thirds vote necessary for ratification. The United States never joined the League of Nations.

More than twenty years later, during World War II (1939–45), Wilson's reputation soared, as he came to be regarded as a wrongly unheeded prophet whose policies would have prevented world calamity. Today the United Nations and collective security pacts are viewed as fulfillment of Wilson's internationalist vision.

Wilson was probably the only president who was a brilliant student and teacher as well as a statesman. Readers of this volume will learn that Wilson was a college professor, president of Princeton University, and author of books on American government. He was also governor of New Jersey. He worked out his political beliefs in the classroom. Then he entered politics to put his theories of government into practice.

Chapter 1
Early Life and Education

Woodrow Wilson was born into a family of Presbyterian ministers and teachers. Naturally enough, the Presbyterian church played a key role in his upbringing. Another important influence as he grew up in the South was his experience of the horrors of the American Civil War. Although he had no formal schooling in his early years, Wilson nevertheless developed passionate interests in literature and politics. By his teens he already envisioned himself as a statesman. First, however, he prepared for the life of an academic. He would eventually become the only president to have earned a PhD.

Family, Childhood, and Schooling

Wilson's grandfather, James Wilson, migrated to the United States from Ulster, Ireland, in 1807. He married Anne Adams, who came on the same ship. James Wilson became a newspaper publisher in Steubenville, Ohio. One of his sons, Joseph Ruggles Wilson, was Woodrow Wilson's father. He became a Presbyterian minister and teacher.

Wilson's mother was Janet (Jessie) Woodrow. She was born in Carlisle, England, just across the border from Scotland. Her father, Thomas Woodrow, was a Scottish Presbyterian minister. In 1836 he brought his family to the United States. In time he settled in Ohio, and there his daughter married and Joseph Ruggles Wilson.

Thomas Woodrow Wilson was born on December 28, 1856, in Staunton, Virginia, where his father was minister of the First Presbyterian Church. Staunton lies along the Shenandoah River, 39 miles (63 kilometers) northwest of Charlottesville. Tommy, as he was called in his childhood, had two older sisters, Marion and Anne. A brother, Joseph Ruggles Wilson Jr., was ten years younger.

Woodrow Wilson's boyhood home is located at 419 Seventh Street in downtown Augusta, Georgia. Today, it is a National Historic Landmark and house museum.

Tommy was a year old when the family moved to Augusta, Georgia. He remembered standing, as a child of four, beside the garden gate and hearing a man say in great excitement that Abraham Lincoln was elected and there was to be war. He ran into the house to ask his father what it meant. He would see a great deal of the destruction and waste from war in the South and learn to hate it. His father, although having grown up in the North, supported some of the South's causes and served during the Civil War as a chaplain with the Confederate army. His church in Augusta was turned into a military hospital.

The Wilson family was happy and affectionate. Tommy and his father were unusually close. Apparently dyslexic from childhood, Tommy did not learn to read until after he was ten and never became a rapid reader. The boy did not go to school until he was thirteen. Until then his father had been his only teacher. Dr. Wilson took the boy on visits to the neighboring cotton gin, corn mill, iron foundry, and ammunition plant and explained how they operated. He taught him

Wilson's father, Joseph, was a minister at the First Presbyterian Church in Augusta. During the Civil War, the church served as a Confederate military hospital.

to look up unfamiliar words in the dictionary and to repeat them until he could use them easily. He taught him how to write simply and express his meaning exactly. This skill with words helped make Wilson famous.

In 1870, when the boy was fourteen, the family moved to Columbia, South Carolina, where his father taught at the Theological Seminary and his uncle, James Woodrow, was the leading light of the seminary faculty. It was a lonely period, and Tommy amused himself by studying nautical terms and writing a fanciful yarn of the sea. He imagined himself to be Admiral Wilson of the United States Navy, whose fleet destroyed a nest of pirates in the South Pacific. The story took the form of daily reports, directed to the Navy Department at Washington, DC.

He began to read books on the science of government. A picture of William Gladstone, prime minister of Great Britain, hung over his desk. He explained to his cousin: "That is Gladstone, the greatest statesman that ever lived. I intend to be a statesman too."

A College Student

In 1873 Wilson entered Davidson College near Charlotte, North Carolina. He was

The Lightfoots

Wilson's interest in parliamentary law began when he was a boy. He organized and made himself president of a club, the Lightfoots, which played baseball and engaged in various secret and adventurous activities. They met in the hayloft of Dr. Wilson's barn. Tommy wrote a constitution for the club and conducted its meetings according to the rules of parliamentary procedure. The boys were impressed with their leader. They would have been more impressed if they had known that their friend would one day write the constitution for the League of Nations.

not prepared for college. By the end of the term his health broke down from overwork. After fifteen months of studying by himself he entered Princeton, then known as the College of New Jersey. Here he discovered the fine qualities of his mind and gained a confidence in himself that he never lost. He studied the art of public speaking and was active in the college debating society. He also edited the college newspaper. In his senior year he wrote a brilliant essay on "Cabinet Government in the United States,"

Nassau Hall, the oldest building at Princeton University, was built in 1756, when the school was still called the College of New Jersey. At the college, Wilson honed his skills in public speaking and debate.

which compared the American government with the British parliamentary system. He dropped the name Thomas and signed himself "Woodrow Wilson."

After his graduation from Princeton in 1879 he entered the University of Virginia to study law. Wilson hoped that law would lead to politics. He earned his law degree in 1882 and entered into a partnership, Renick and Wilson, in Atlanta, Georgia. A brief struggle to build up a practice convinced him that he would never make a successful lawyer.

Woodrow Wilson

Wilson is pictured here as a young man. After graduating from Princeton in 1879, he earned a law degree at the University of Virginia in Charlottesville and a PhD at Johns Hopkins University in Baltimore, Maryland.

He abandoned his law career and returned to the "advantages and delights of study" in 1883.

This time he spent two years at Johns Hopkins University studying history and political science. For all his brilliance, Wilson never stood at the top of his class. He refused to study subjects that bored him, and he had great contempt for the pursuit of high marks and academic degrees. He took his degree of doctor of philosophy from Johns Hopkins in 1886 only at the insistence of friends who pointed out that it meant a higher salary as a teacher. His dissertation was also his first book, *Congressional Government: A Study in American Politics*, which was published in 1885. In this penetrating study he made the point that congressional government, as practiced in the United States, divides responsibility and thus lends itself to inefficiency and corruption. He suggested reforms that would make the American system more effective and more answerable to public opinion.

Chapter 2

A Professor, University President, and Governor

Wilson was a professional academic before he entered politics. He spent twenty-five years as a college professor and administrator, winning recognition for his bold reforms while serving as president of Princeton. His built on his reputation as a reformer as he made the transition to politics, gaining national notice as a progressive governor of New Jersey.

College Professor

Wilson was twenty-nine years old when he started on his career as an educator. He was an associate professor of history at Bryn Mawr College (for women) (1885–88) and then a professor of history and political economy

A Professor, University President, and Governor

at Wesleyan University, in Middletown, Connecticut (1888–90). In 1890 he returned to the College of New Jersey as a professor of jurisprudence (the science of law) and political economy. In the next twenty years he would play a leading role as the school grew into the great Princeton University. For eight years (1902–10) he served as president of the university.

Year after year the students at Princeton elected Wilson their most popular professor. He was an inspiring teacher. He had small respect for the kind of mind that accumulates facts and dates. He believed, instead, in the importance of "developing the mind by using it rather than stuffing it." "The essence of the cultured mind is its capacity for relating knowledge," he declared.

They were busy years. In addition to teaching he published *Congressional Government*

> Wilson returned to Princeton as a professor of jurisprudence. As president of Princeton from 1902 to 1910, he upgraded the university both financially and academically.

21

(1885), *The State* (1889), *Division and Reunion* (1893), *George Washington* (1896), *A History of the American People* (1902), and *Constitutional Government in the United States* (1908). He wrote many essays and book reviews and was in great demand as a lecturer.

Wilson was always overworked and suffered repeated sick spells, which required long periods of rest. Historians have suspected that he suffered perhaps as many as three strokes—two minor and one more serious—during the 1890s. In 1906 he was told that he must retire and lead a very quiet life, but he kept on going. Without the help and sympathy of his wife, he could never have accomplished all that he did.

Marriage and Family Life

Wilson had married Ellen Axson of Rome, Georgia, in 1885. They had three daughters—Margaret (born in 1886), Jessie (1887), and Eleanor (1889). His wife made sure that he had quiet during his working hours, freedom from money worries, and the frequent association of intellectual friends. On the small salary of a teacher

Wilson married Ellen Louise Axson in June 1885. As a teenager, Ellen had studied painting and planned to become a professional artist. After her daughters were born, Ellen dedicated herself to her family.

they managed to help their younger relatives get a college education by opening their home to them.

A friend of the Wilsons' in later years wrote, "The more I am with the Wilsons the more I am struck by their unrivaled home life. I have never dreamed such sweetness and love could be."

PRINCETON UNIVERSITY PRESIDENT

As president of Princeton, Wilson launched his first reform crusade—to build a university that would produce leaders and statesmen. The first problem was to get rid of the upperclass "eating clubs." "The side-shows are swallowing up the circus," he remarked. The second was to establish a stronger graduate college. He proposed a plan in which graduates and undergraduates should live together in small colleges presided over by teachers and tutors. Students and professors would benefit by the mutual stimulation of cultured, scholarly ideals.

Wilson succeeded in reorganizing the courses of study and in adding forty-seven young scholars to the faculty, called preceptors.

A Professor, University President, and Governor

Their duty was to individually supervise the students and to develop small discussion groups. But on the major issues he failed.

Students and alumni opposed elimination of social clubs. A group in the faculty was determined to place the graduate college under a separate administration and to house its students in a quadrangle far removed from the undergraduate campus, libraries, and

Wilson, holding his hat in his hand, is pictured here as a student with other members of the Alligators eating club at Princeton. Later, as Princeton's president, Wilson tried to abolish eating clubs because he believed that they unfairly divided students by social class.

Wilson's Controversial Legacy at Princeton

In 1930 Princeton University created the School of Public and International Affairs, according to the school's website, "in the spirit of Woodrow Wilson's interest in preparing students for leadership in public and international affairs." It was an interdisciplinary program, meaning that it combined multiple subject areas, within the undergraduate liberal arts college. A graduate school program was established in 1948, and the school was renamed the Woodrow Wilson School of Public and International Affairs to honor the thirteenth president of Princeton and the twenty-eighth president of the United States. The school continues a long Princeton tradition of teaching a broad range of students from around the world in such fields as politics, economics, sociology, psychology, and the physical sciences. Many of these students seek careers in public service, especially in foreign relations.

In November 2015 students at the Woodrow Wilson School of Public and International Affairs and others at Princeton launched protests to call attention to Wilson's racist and segregationist views. They demanded that the university drop Wilson's name and imagery from the school, add cultural diversity to its core curriculum, and establish a safe space for minorities. They also called for a required cultural-competency training program for professors and instructors. Some Princeton professors agreed that there should be a debate on campus about Wilson's legacy.

University leaders studied the protesters' requests and investigated Wilson's views and Princeton's state of race relations on campus. They decided that

Wilson's achievements deserved to be honored as long as his flaws were also recognized and discussed, adding that some of Wilson's ideas "clearly contradict with the values we hold today." Specific concerns were "the position he took as Princeton's president to prevent the enrollment of black students and the policies he instituted as US president that resulted in the re-segregation of the federal civil service." The university leaders promised to make changes, such as encouraging more minority students to earn doctoral degrees and expanding campus symbols and art to be culturally inclusive. On the same day that Princeton's leaders announced their decision to keep Wilson's name on the school, the school introduced an exhibit that put Wilson in the context of his times and explained his faults.

laboratories. Wilson was convinced that such plans reduced the graduate college to little more than an expensive hall of residence. When two alumni willed several million dollars to the graduate college on condition that the opposition's plans be carried out, Wilson was defeated. He felt that the issue was between democracy and the power of money and special privilege.

Workers' Compensation Act

One of Woodrow Wilson's early achievements as governor of New Jersey was signing into law the Workers' Compensation Act on April 4, 1911. Prior to the law's enactment, New Jersey prohibited workers who were injured at their jobs from receiving any money for medical expenses from employers, even if another worker caused the accident.

The state established an Employers' Liability Commission to study the workplace injury laws and to suggest improvements. The commission stated that "compensation to injured workmen is a legitimate charge against the cost of manufacture" and that workers should receive fair compensation for injuries sustained while working.

The Workers' Compensation Act created a no-fault method of guaranteed medical care for injured workers, short-term wage relief, and a benefit plan for permanent disabilities. It also required payments for the dependents of workers who were killed while performing their jobs. In return, workers surrendered their right to sue their employers for further payments, other than in cases of deliberate injuries. New Jersey was the first US state to enact such a program.

Governor of New Jersey

The Princeton battle attracted wide publicity and the attention of conservative kingmakers in the Democratic Party, who offered Wilson the 1910 nomination for governor of New Jersey. Wilson resigned from the university, and, artfully turning the tables on his patrons, he won the governorship with a dynamic, progressive campaign.

During his time as New Jersey governor, Wilson (*standing*) poses with (*from left to right*) his daughter Jessie; wife, Ellen; and daughters Margaret and Eleanor. Wilson served as governor from 1911 to 1913.

As governor, Wilson showed his independence and his capacity for getting things done. Again, as at Princeton, he plunged into battle with forces he was convinced opposed the public good. New Jersey was run by a group of political bosses who thought they could use Wilson as a respectable front. He sidestepped the Democratic Party machine and appealed directly to the voters for support of his program. In a little over a year he put through a public utility control act, a corrupt political practices act, a workers' compensation act, and a direct primary act.

Chapter 3
The Twenty-eighth President

Wilson's bold reforms as New Jersey governor attracted national attention to the college president turned politician. In 1912 he won the Democratic Party's nomination for president of the United States. Former president Theodore Roosevelt's bolt to the Progressive Party had split the Republican Party, a factor that allowed Wilson to be elected with only 42 percent of the popular vote. The electoral vote was 435 for Wilson, 88 for Roosevelt, and 8 for incumbent Republican president William Howard Taft. In his campaign Wilson had answered Roosevelt's call for a "New Nationalism" with his own equally compelling vision of a "New Freedom." Wilson was the first Southern-born president elected since the Civil War.

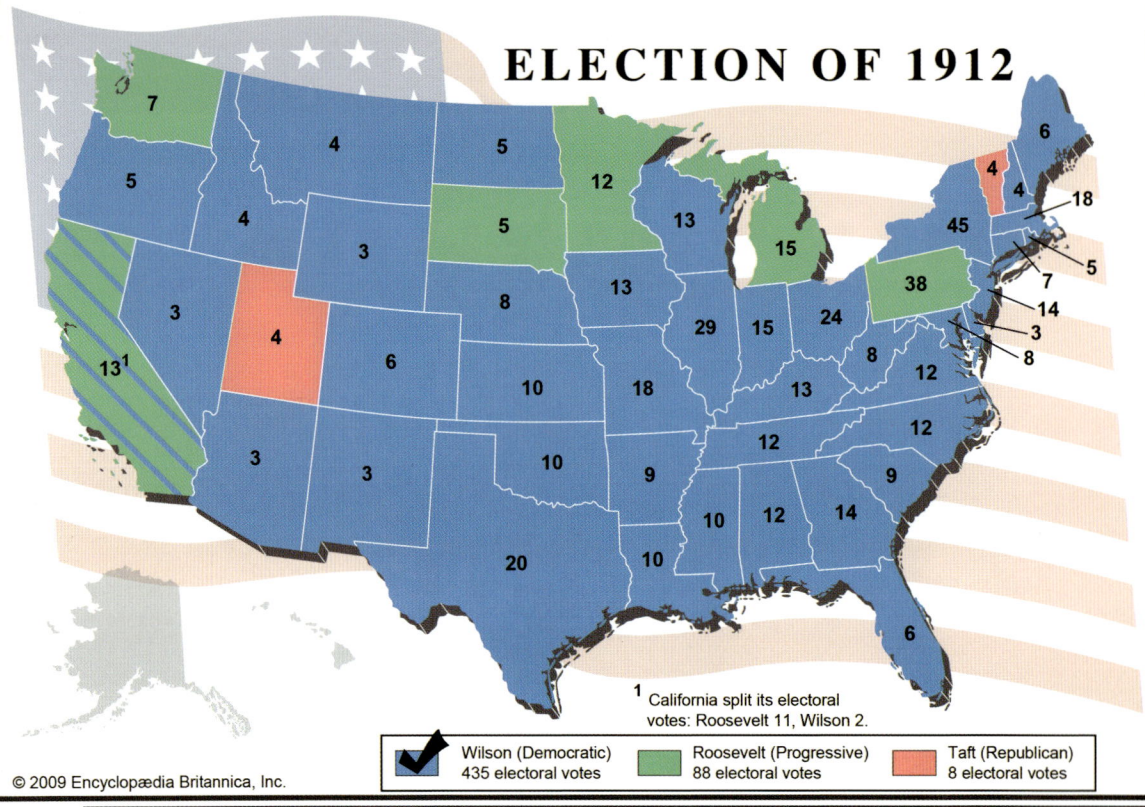

Wilson, a Democrat, claimed an overwhelming victory in the 1912 presidential election. He won all the states in blue on the map.

LIFE IN THE WHITE HOUSE

The Wilson family was far from happy about the prospect of going to the White House. The outgoing president, William Howard Taft, said to them, "I'm glad to be going—this is the lonesomest place in the world." Eleanor Wilson wrote in her memoirs that the day before her father's inauguration she

The Twenty-eighth President

wept until she was exhausted, crying, "It will kill them—it will kill them both."

Yet the Wilson family adapted themselves very quickly to life in the White House. Ellen Wilson made a simple and democratic home, as she had done wherever they went. Two weddings took place in the White House in the first two years. Jessie married Francis B. Sayre on November 26, 1913, and Eleanor married William Gibbs McAdoo on May 7, 1914.

Ellen Wilson's health began to fail early in 1914. Her ability to endear herself to everyone

President Wilson speaks at his first inauguration on the east portico of the US Capitol in Washington, DC, on March 4, 1913.

was indicated by an action of Congress. Informed that she was sinking, legislators hastily passed a bill for slum clearance in Washington, which she had very much at heart, so that she might be told of it before she died, in August of that year.

Dependent as he had always been on his wife's companionship, the president became lonely and depressed. Through his personal physician, Colonel Cary Grayson, he met a beautiful and gracious widow, Edith Bolling Galt. The two were married in December 1915.

Political Reform During the First Term

Wilson called his philosophy of government the "new freedom." "What I am interested in is having the government of the United States more concerned about human rights than about property rights," he declared. Convinced that strong executive leadership was necessary for progress, he went further than any other president in forcing his wishes on Congress. He called Congress in an extra session early in April 1913 and addressed the two houses in person. This broke a precedent of long standing. From time to time after that he went before Congress with parts of his program.

The result was a mass of progressive legislation unequaled in any administration up to that time. Wilson succeeded during his first term in pushing through a number of meaningful measures: tariff reduction, banking regulations, antitrust legislation, beneficial farmer-labor enactments, and highway construction using state grants-in-aid. Wilson's New Freedom program actually included most of the progressive proposals of his main 1912 presidential opponent, Theodore Roosevelt. The program was notable for its extensive use of federal power to protect the common people.

Tariff Reform

The Underwood-Simmons Tariff Act of 1913 lowered duties on more than a hundred items and reduced average tariff rates from 40 percent to 25 percent. It was the first time duties on imports had been reduced in forty years. A tariff commission was established in 1916 to study tariffs and make recommendations.

Income Tax

To offset the loss in revenue from tariff reductions, a graduated income tax law was enacted as authorized by the newly adopted Sixteenth Amendment to the Constitution. It was levied according to wealth.

Currency and Credit Reform

After months of debate and bargaining over banking and currency reform, in 1913 Congress passed the act creating the Federal Reserve banking system, which remains the most powerful government agency in economic matters. The Federal Reserve System issued a flexible new currency—Federal Reserve notes—based on gold and commercial paper. The Federal Reserve Act also provided for a board of presidential appointees to supervise the system. For the first time in American history, finance and credits were placed under government direction. Another law, the Federal Farm Loan Act of 1916, created twelve farm loan banks to give cheap and easy credit to farmers and tenants.

The Twenty-eighth President

Top: This ten-dollar banknote was issued by the state of South Carolina in the late nineteenth century. *Bottom*: This is today's ten-dollar Federal Reserve note. In 1913 Congress passed and Wilson approved the Federal Reserve Act, which created a central US banking system to oversee the supply of currency.

37

Regulation of Business

The Federal Trade Commission was created through the Federal Trade Commission Act of 1914. It had the power to forbid unfair business practices that would lead to monopoly. The Clayton Antitrust Act (1914), designed to strengthen the Sherman Antitrust Act (1890), defined the methods of competition that the Commission was empowered to forbid. It made officers of corporations liable for illegal acts of those corporations, exempted labor unions from antitrust acts, and forbade the use of labor injunctions except where necessary to protect property. In addition, the act legalized peaceful strikes, picketing, and boycotting.

Joseph E. Davies became the first chairman of the Federal Trade Commission after its establishment in 1914. He had previously served as commissioner of corporations and had helped get Wilson elected in 1912.

The Twenty-eighth President

A cartoon from 1914 depicts President Wilson priming a pump. Wilson's agenda to stimulate growth in the US economy included laws to regulate currency with the Federal Reserve System, improve the tariff system, and establish antitrust laws.

39

WILSON'S RACIAL VIEWS

Wilson's first term also had an ugly side. Despite his Southern birth and upbringing, the president held racial views that mirrored the then prevailing indifference of white Northerners toward injustices inflicted on African Americans. Several of Wilson's Cabinet members were Southerners, however, and they demanded that segregation be introduced into the federal government. Wilson permitted such efforts to go forward. Protests by the recently formed National Association for the Advancement of Colored People (NAACP) compelled the administration to drop some of the most obvious discriminatory measures, such as "white" and "colored" restrooms. Some Northern Democrats and Republican Progressives, whose support Wilson valued, had also raised objections, and practical problems arose in separating the races in the workplace.

Taken together, those protests, objections, and problems prompted the administration to stage a partial formal retreat while maintaining much of the substance of segregation. In a similar vein, the numbers and percentages of African Americans in the federal workforce were sharply reduced—a practice that continued under Northern-dominated Republican administrations in the 1920s. Wilson further soured his relations with African Americans by permitting a well-publicized White House screening of D. W. Griffith's artistically ambitious but clearly racist film *The Birth of a Nation* (1915). (The only move Wilson made toward improving race relations would come in July 1918, during his second term, when he eloquently but belatedly condemned lynching.)

Foreign Affairs

Foreign affairs bedeviled Wilson from his first days in the White House. Latin America was the first trouble spot. Then, in the summer of 1914, all Europe was plunged into war.

Latin America

Congress in 1912 had enacted a Panama tolls law that violated the Hay-Pauncefote Treaty of 1901 with Great Britain, guaranteeing equal treatment in the use of the Panama Canal. Wilson persuaded Congress to repeal the act.

American businessmen were investing heavily in the mines, railroads, and other resources of Latin America. Wilson announced soon after his inauguration that he would abandon "dollar diplomacy." This policy meant that investors could no longer expect the United States government to protect their interests. Nevertheless, Wilson permitted US intervention to restore order in Nicaragua, Haiti, and the Dominican Republic.

In 1914 the US Marines seized the port of Veracruz, Mexico, when Mexican police arrested several American sailors. Mediation by the "A B C powers" (Argentina, Brazil,

Mexican revolutionary Pancho Villa led his followers on a raid into New Mexico in 1916. President Wilson ordered an expedition to catch him, but it did not succeed.

and Chile) prevented war. In March 1916 a Mexican rebel, Pancho Villa, raided Columbus, New Mexico, killing seventeen Americans. With the permission of President Venustiano Carranza of Mexico, the United States sent an expedition into Mexico under General John J. Pershing. They failed to catch Villa and were withdrawn in January 1917. Wilson eventually reconciled himself to a hands-off stance toward Mexico.

The War in Europe

The outbreak of World War I in August 1914, which coincided with his first wife's death, tried President Wilson's mind and soul. Almost no one questioned American neutrality in the beginning, but both the British blockade of maritime trade and German U-boat attacks soon made neutrality painful. On May 7, 1915, when a U-boat sank the British liner *Lusitania*, killing nearly 1,200 people, including 128 Americans, the war came home with a vengeance.

Wilson at first urged his countrymen to show restraint, declaring, "There is such a thing as a man being too proud to fight," but he also pressed the Germans to rein in their

The *Lusitania*

The *Lusitania* was a British ocean liner built in the early twentieth century to carry passengers across the Atlantic Ocean. In May 1915, during World War I, the *Lusitania* was returning from New York City to Liverpool, England, with 1,959 passengers and crew on board. The British Admiralty warned the *Lusitania*'s captain that current reports showed German submarine activity in the area and that the ship should either avoid the area or use evasive tactics such as zigzagging — changing course every few minutes at irregular intervals — to confuse any attempt by U-boats to plot the ship's course for torpedoing. The ship's captain chose to ignore these recommendations, and on the afternoon of May 7 a torpedo struck and exploded on the ship's starboard side. A heavier explosion followed, possibly caused by damage to the ship's steam engines and pipes. Within 20 minutes the *Lusitania* had sunk, and 1,198 people were drowned, including 128 US citizens.

The loss of the liner and so many of its passengers aroused a wave of indignation in the United States. It was fully expected that a declaration of war would follow, but the US government clung to its policy of neutrality. The Germans, who had circulated warnings that the *Lusitania* would be sunk, felt themselves fully justified in attacking a vessel that was furthering the war aims of their enemy (besides passengers, the ship was carrying rifle ammunition and shells). On May 13, 1915, the US government sent a note to the German government condemning their submarine war policies, but this note and two following ones constituted the immediate limit of US reaction to the *Lusitania* incident. Later, however, the United States would cite German submarine warfare as a justification for American entry into the war.

The front page of the *New York Times* of May 8, 1915, reports the sinking of the *Lusitania*.

submarines and decided to build up the armed forces. Those moves impelled Secretary of State William Jennings Bryan to resign in protest and to oppose Wilson politically. A combination of patience and firmness on the president's part paid off when the Germans, for military reasons of their own, pledged to curtail submarine warfare in April 1916. For the rest of that year the threat of war receded, while relations with Great Britain worsened because of their ever-tightening blockade and their brutal suppression of the Easter Rising, the armed revolt in Ireland that eventually led to independence.

Chapter 4

A Second Term and the Great War

Wilson was elected to a second term in 1916, becoming the first Democratic president to win a second consecutive term since Andrew Jackson in 1828. He defeated the Republican candidate Charles Evans Hughes by an electoral vote of 277 to 254. The campaign cry "He kept us out of war" helped, but Wilson's domestic record on progressive and labor issues played the biggest part in his victory. During his second term, however, the war would come to dominate Wilson's presidency. After the United States finally declared war in 1917, Wilson proved to be a surprisingly effective war president.

This button is from Wilson's 1916 presidential campaign. Pictured with him is former New York governor Martin H. Glynn (*right*), who gave the keynote speech at the 1916 Democratic National Convention.

War Approaches

After the election Wilson mounted a peace offensive aimed at ending the war. First he made a public diplomatic appeal to the warring countries to state their peace terms and accept American mediation. Then on January 22, 1917, he gave a stirring speech in which he called for a "peace without victory" and pledged to establish a league of nations to prevent future wars.

Unfortunately, the Germans undermined Wilson's peace efforts by unleashing their submarines on February 1. For the next two months Wilson agonized over how to respond. Public opinion remained divided and uncertain, even after publication of the Zimmermann Telegram, a secret communication by the German foreign secretary that offered Texas, New Mexico, and Arizona to Mexico in return for going to war against the United States. Wilson finally decided to intervene, mainly because he could see no alternative and hoped to use American power as a means to build a just, lasting peace. On April 2, 1917, he went before Congress to ask for a declaration of war so that the United States could strive to fulfill his declaration that "the world must be made safe for democracy." Congress approved the war resolution quickly, and Wilson signed it on April 6, 1917.

A Call to Arms

Generally speaking, the efforts at mobilization went through two stages. During the

On April 2, 1917, President Wilson asked Congress to declare war on Germany.

first, lasting roughly from April to December 1917, the administration relied mainly on voluntary and cooperative efforts. During the second stage, after December 1917, the government moved rapidly to establish complete control over every important phase of economic life. Railroads were nationalized; a war industries board established ironclad controls over industry; food and fuel were strictly rationed; an emergency-fleet corporation began construction of a vast merchant fleet; and a war labor board used pressure to prevent strikes.

Wilson's Support for Women's Suffrage

As the United States joined World War I in Europe, the long-running movement for women's suffrage heated up at home. In 1917 a group of suffragists protested at the White House to demand a constitutional amendment that would give women the right to vote. Some of the women chained themselves to a White House fence to draw attention to their cause.

At first Wilson seemed not to take the suffragists seriously. He began to change his opinion, however, after some of the protesters were jailed and beaten. He became a champion of their cause and admitted that the country had a debt to pay to them, especially after they had been asked to support their husbands and sons fighting abroad and to help with the war effort at home.

On September 30, 1918, President Wilson gave a speech before the US Senate in support of the Nineteenth Amendment, which would guarantee women the right to vote. The House of Representatives had already approved the amendment, but the Senate had not yet voted on it. In his address Wilson told the Senate, "we have made partners of the women in this war ... Shall we admit them only to a partnership of suffering and sacrifice and toil and not to a partnership of privilege and right?" Unfortunately, Wilson's inspiring words fell on deaf ears, and the bill died in the Senate, two votes short of passage.

A year later another congressional vote took place. The Nineteenth Amendment passed in the House of Representatives on May 21, 1919, and in the Senate on June 4. After three-fourths of the states had ratified the amendment, it was proclaimed on August 26, 1920, as part of the Constitution of the United States.

Alison Turnbull Hopkins holds a banner that reads, "Mr. President How Long Must Women Wait for Liberty," as she pickets for women's suffrage outside the White House in 1917.

FEED a FIGHTER

Eat only what you need —
Waste nothing —
That he and his family
may have enough

A poster promotes voluntary food rationing in support of the US war effort during World War I.

Opposition to the war was sternly suppressed under the Espionage Act of 1917. At the same time, the Committee on Public Information, headed by the progressive journalist George Creel, mobilized publicists, scholars, and others in a vast prowar propaganda effort. The words of Wilson reached the German people by radio for the first time in history. Leaflets were scattered from airplanes, shot from guns and rockets, and smuggled behind the enemy lines. Wilson said that this was a "war to end war." He spoke of "peace without victory" and without revenge.

America's Role in the War

The American military contribution, while small compared to that of the Allies during the entire war, was in two respects decisive in the outcome. The US Navy, fully prepared at the outset, provided the ships that helped the British overcome the submarine threat by the autumn of 1917. The US Army, some four million men strong, was raised mainly by conscription (the draft) under the Selective Service Act of 1917. The American Expeditionary Force of more than 1.2 million men under General

SPIRIT of 1917

JOIN THE
UNITED STATES MARINES
AND BE
FIRST IN DEFENSE ON LAND OR SEA
APPLY AT

A recruitment poster from 1917 displays a US Marine Corps color guard leading an advance.

Pershing reached France by September 1918. This huge boost in manpower tipped the scales against the Germans and helped to end the war in November 1918, a year earlier than military planners had anticipated.

The Battle for the Peace Treaty

On January 8, 1918, Wilson had announced his Fourteen Points as the basis for a peace settlement. They were more than peace terms; they were terms for a better world. He followed this speech with his famous

(From left to right) Italian prime minister Vittorio Orlando, British prime minister David Lloyd George, French premier Georges Clemenceau, and US president Woodrow Wilson meet at the peace conference in Paris in 1919.

"self-determination" speech on February 11 in which he said: "National aspirations must be respected; people may now be dominated and governed only by their own consent. 'Self determination' is not a mere phrase; it is an imperative principle of action ... "

Later that year, the German proposals for peace came in the midst of congressional elections. Wilson appealed to the people to support his policies by returning a Democratic majority to both houses. The party was defeated, however, and with a Republican majority in control he was no longer able to lead the Congress.

Against the advice of those close to him, the president decided to attend the peace conference in Paris and fight for his policies in person. He took with him few advisers, none from the Republican Party. On December 13, 1918, he arrived in Europe. Probably no man has ever been given such an ovation. Wherever he went enormous crowds gathered, sobbing, cheering, shouting his name.

The peace conference dragged on week after weary week, and Wilson spent seven months in difficult negotiations. David

Lloyd George of England, Vittorio Orlando of Italy, and Georges Clemenceau of France were experienced and shrewd diplomats, and each was determined to have his own way. The endless arguing and the official receptions and banquets frayed Wilson's nerves. He suffered a brief but severe illness. Thereafter he was more tense, nervous, and irritable.

THE TREATY OF VERSAILLES

The peace treaty was given to the German delegation to sign at Versailles (a town near Paris) on May 7, 1919. The German delegates strongly objected to its severe terms, which they said were not consistent with Wilson's Fourteen Points. The Allies made only small concessions. Finally, on June 28, 1919, the German delegates signed in the Hall of Mirrors in the Palace of Versailles. The treaty took force on January 10, 1920. A treaty with Austria was signed on September 10, 1919, at St-Germain. Treaties were signed with Bulgaria at Neuilly on November 27, 1919, and with the Ottoman Empire at Sèvres on August 10, 1920.

A painting by William Orpen depicts the signing of the peace treaty at the Palace of Versailles on June 28, 1919. Wilson (*seated in the front row holding documents*) fought hard for the terms of the treaty.

The peace treaty as agreed on in June 1919 contained many of Wilson's ideas. His greatest success was in writing into the Versailles Treaty the Covenant (constitution) of a League of Nations. On July 10, 1919, he laid it before a hostile Senate, led by Henry Cabot Lodge and a "little group of willful men," as

Wilson called them. Lodge and his fellow Republicans were especially opposed to the League of Nations, but Wilson refused to compromise his dream. In search of popular support that would overwhelm the Senate, he toured the country in defense of the League. Exhausted, he collapsed in Pueblo, Colorado, late in September. A stroke left him paralyzed.

For a month only his wife and his doctor were allowed to see him. Then, with his wife guiding his hand, he placed a wobbly signature on major bills. When Secretary of State Robert Lansing presumed to call Cabinet meetings, Wilson promptly dismissed him. He refused to let his vice president, Thomas R. Marshall, take charge. In her memoirs Edith Wilson said that the president remained the active head of state, making decisions on the basis of digests that she had prepared.

The president's illness, which disabled him for several months, increased his inflexibility concerning the Lodge reservations. With equal stubbornness, Lodge refused to consent to any compromise. The result was failure to obtain the necessary two-thirds majority for ratification when the Senate voted on the treaty on November 19, 1919, and again on March 19, 1920.

President Wilson, seated at his desk, signs documents sometime after his stroke, which left him partially paralyzed on his left side. His wife, Edith, helps to hold down the paperwork.

The Woodrow Wilson House

The home that Wilson and his wife lived in after they left the White House became a property of the National Trust for Historic Preservation upon Edith Wilson's death in 1961. It opened as a museum in 1963 and was named a National Historic Landmark in 1964. The museum spotlights President Wilson's years in Washington, from 1912 until his death in 1924. Architect Waddy Butler Wood designed the Georgian Revival–style house and gardens, which were finished in 1915. The home has been preserved as it looked in 1924, with furniture, photographs, artwork, gifts, and personal items of the president and his wife. The drawing room features a Steinway piano that Wilson brought from the White House.

On November 10, 1923, Wilson addressed the American public by radio from this house on the eve of the fifth anniversary of Armistice Day—the day of the signing of the armistice ending World War I. This was the first live remote radio address to be broadcast nationally. Still stung by the country's refusal to join the League of Nations, Wilson used his four-minute speech to urge Americans to support an active role for the United States in international affairs.

The 1920 Presidential Election

In the 1920 election Wilson called for "a great and solemn referendum" on the treaty and the League of Nations and entertained fantasies about running on that issue himself. Edith Wilson and his closest friends quietly put an end to those notions. Instead, the Democrats nominated James M. Cox, the governor of Ohio, on the strength of his lack of association with Wilson. The Republican candidate was Warren G. Harding, a senator who had opposed the League of Nations. Harding called for a return to "normalcy" and blamed all the country's troubles on Wilson. The Republicans won a landslide victory, which they interpreted as a mandate to reverse Wilson's progressive policies at home and his internationalism abroad.

Wilson's Later Years

Wilson lived at 2340 S Street NW in Washington, DC, for almost three years after leaving office in March 1921. Though an invalid, he never wavered in his conviction that the United States should and would eventually join the League of Nations, and he took a keen interest in politics. In one of his last public appearances he rode in the funeral procession of his younger and supposedly healthy successor, Harding. Wilson died in his sleep in his Washington home on February 3, 1924. His remains were interred in the newly begun National Cathedral in Washington, DC. He is the only president buried in the capital city.

In 1921, Wilson is steadied by a servant at the doorway of his home in Washington, DC.

CONCLUSION

In 1919, while President Wilson was still in office, the Norwegian Nobel Committee awarded him the Nobel Prize for Peace. He was honored with the prize because of his efforts to create the League of Nations. Because Wilson was too ill to deliver his acceptance speech in person, he asked Albert G. Schmederman, US minister to Norway, to accept the prize on his behalf. Wilson thanked the committee for honoring him and said, in part,

> *If there were but one such prize, or if this were to be the last, I could not of course accept it. For mankind has not yet been rid of the unspeakable horror of war. I am convinced that our generation has, despite its wounds, made notable progress. But it is the better part of wisdom to consider our work as one begun. It will be a continuing labor. In the indefinite course of [the] years before us there will be abundant opportunity for others to distinguish themselves in the crusade against hate and fear and war.*

Wilson was given the Peace Prize despite the fact that he failed to bring the United

F. Graham Cootes painted the official portrait of President Wilson in 1936. Today, it hangs above the Grand Staircase in the White House.

States into the League of Nations. This was his most bitter disappointment. Wilson's historical reputation at first suffered from his failure to carry the day in his last years and the ascendancy of the Republicans. It declined further during the 1930s with the "revisionist" disgust against World War I. But during World War II (1939–45) Wilson's stature improved, as many Americans came to believe that his policies, if heeded, could have prevented the conflict.

The establishment of the United Nations (UN) after World War is considered an achievement of Wilson's internationalist idea. The successor to the League of Nations, the UN is dedicated to resolving international disputes without war. Another enduring aspect of Wilson's internationalism is his idea that US foreign policy should promote democracy around the globe. The notion that the United States should try to influence foreign governments was a new approach to international relations that continues to play a role in US policy today.

Glossary

autonomy The power or right of self-government.

calamity An event that causes great harm.

diplomacy The work of keeping up relations between the governments of different countries.

discrimination The practice of treating some people better than others without any fair or proper reason.

dyslexic Having dyslexia, a learning disability marked by difficulties in reading, spelling, and writing.

exempt To free or release from some requirement that others must meet or deal with.

inauguration An act or ceremony that puts someone into office.

inflict To cause (something damaging or painful) to be endured, as in to inflict a punishment.

injunction A court order commanding or forbidding the doing of some act. Labor injunctions have been used to restrict the actions of unions and to prevent workers from going on strike.

integrity The quality or state of being complete or undivided.

liberal arts The studies, such as literature, philosophy, languages, or history, in a college or university intended to develop the mind in a general way rather than give professional or vocational skills.

monopoly Complete control over the entire supply of goods or a service in a certain market.

oratory The art of speaking in public skillfully and powerfully.

parliamentary law The rules governing the meetings of legislatures and other organizations, such as associations and clubs.

penetrating Acute or discerning.

precedent An earlier occurrence of something similar; something that may serve as an example or rule to be followed in the future.

propaganda Ideas or statements that are often false or exaggerated and that are spread to help a cause, a political leader, or a government.

public utility A company, such as an electric company, that provides a public service and must follow special rules made by the government.
ratification Legal or official approval.
segregation The separation or isolation of a race, class, or group.
seminary A school for the training of priests, ministers, or rabbis.
socialist One who advocates socialism, a way of organizing a society in which people live in cooperation with one another and everyone who contributes to the production of a good is entitled to a share in it.
stroke Sudden weakening or loss of consciousness or the power to feel or move caused by the breaking or blocking (as by a clot) of a blood vessel in the brain.

For More Information

Miller Center of Public Affairs
PO Box 400406
Charlottesville, VA 22904
(434) 924-7236
Website: http://millercenter.org
This organization at the University of Virginia focuses on the study of US presidents, American political history, and public policy. Its website provides information about the life, times, and achievements of Woodrow Wilson (http://millercenter.org/president/wilson).

The National World War I Museum and Memorial
100 West 26th Street
Kansas City, MO 64108
(816) 888-8100

For More Information

Website: https://www.theworldwar.org
This museum and memorial commemorates the Great War by exploring the issues behind the conflict, its battles, and its effect worldwide.

Office of the Historian
US Department of State
(202) 955-0200
Website: https://history.state.gov
The Office of the Historian, part of the US Department of State, provides a wealth of information about the history of US foreign policy. Its website includes material on the League of Nations (https://history.state.gov/milestones/1914-1920/league).

Woodrow Wilson Center
One Woodrow Wilson Plaza
1300 Pennsylvania Avenue NW
Washington, DC 20004-3027
(202) 691-4000
Website: https://www.wilsoncenter.org
The Woodrow Wilson Center was chartered by the US Congress as the official memorial to President Wilson. The institution deals with global issues and policy

through independent research by scholars from around the world.

Woodrow Wilson House
2340 S Street NW
Washington, DC 20008
(202) 387-4062
Website: http://www.woodrowwilsonhouse.org
Owned by the National Trust for Historic Preservation, Wilson's former home operates as a museum today. Its collections and exhibits focus on Wilson's Washington years (1912–1924).

Woodrow Wilson Presidential Library and Museum
20 North Coalter Street
Staunton, VA 24401
(540) 885-0897
Website: http://www.woodrowwilson.org
The Woodrow Wilson Presidential Library and Museum provides access to Wilson-related documents and artifacts, either online or in person. Located next to Wilson's birthplace, the museum includes information about his family, his years at Princeton, his New Jersey governorship, and his years as president, with special

emphasis on World War I and the League of Nations.

Woodrow Wilson School of Public and
    International Affairs
Robertson Hall
Princeton University
Princeton, NJ 08544-1013
(609) 258-8909 [Public Affairs and
    Communications]
Website: http://wws.princeton.edu
This school at Princeton offers undergraduate and graduate studies for people who are interested in public policy.

WEBSITES

Because of the changing nature of internet links, Rosen Publishing has developed an online list of Web sites related to the subject of this book. This site is updated regularly. Please use this link to access the list:

http://www.rosenlinks.com/PPPL/wilson

For Further Reading

Ashby, Ruth. *Woodrow & Edith Wilson*. Milwaukee, WI: World Almanac Library, 2005.

Auchincloss, Louis. *Woodrow Wilson: A Life*. New York, NY: Penguin Books, 2009.

Bozonelis, Helen Koutras. *A Look at the Nineteenth Amendment: Women Win the Right to Vote*. Berkeley Heights, NJ: Enslow Publishers, 2009.

Day, Meredith, and Colleen Adams. *A Primary Source Investigation of Women's Suffrage* (Uncovering American History). New York, NY: Rosen Publishing, 2016.

Hosein, Ann, ed. *Key Figures of World War I* (Biographies of War). New York, NY: Britannica Educational Publishing, 2016.

For Further Reading

Hyde, Natalie. *World War I: The Cause for War* (World War I, Remembering the Great War). New York, NY: Crabtree Publishing Company, 2014.

Kenney, Karen Latchana, and Edward G. Lengel. *Everything World War I*. Washington, DC: National Geographic Society, 2014.

Kent, Zachary. *World War I: From the Lusitania to Versailles* (United States at War). Berkeley Heights, NJ: Enslow Publishers, 2011.

Lanser, Amanda. *World War I through the Eyes of Woodrow Wilson*. Minneapolis, MN: Core Library, 2016.

Marsico, Katie. *Woodrow Wilson* (Presidents and their Times). Tarrytown, NY: Marshall Cavendish, 2011.

Otfinoski, Steven. *The Sinking of the Lusitania: An Interactive History Adventure* (You Choose Books). North Mankato, MN: Capstone Press, 2014.

Oxlade, Chris. *World War I* (Secret History). Mankato, MN: Arcturus Publishing, 2010.

Powley, Adam. *World War I Close Up* (The War Chronicles). New York, NY: Rosen Publishing, 2016.

Rumsch, BreAnn. *Woodrow Wilson*. Edina, MN: ABDO, 2009.

Steele, Philip. *Did Anything Good Come Out of World War I?* (Innovation through Adversity). New York, NY: Rosen Publishing, 2015.

Swayze, Alan. *The End of World War I: The Treaty of Versailles and Its Tragic Legacy*. New York, NY: Crabtree Publishing, 2014.

Wilson, John. *Failed Hope: The Story of the Lost Peace*. Toronto, ON: Dundurn Press, 2012.

Index

A

"ABC powers," 42–43
Adams, Anne, 12
Augusta, GA, 13, 14

B

Birth of a Nation, The (1915), 41
Bryan, William Jennings, Secretary of State, 45
Bryn Mawr College, 20

C

"Cabinet Government in the United States," 16
Carranza, Venustiano, President of Mexico, 43
Civil War, 11, 13–14, 31
Clayton Antitrust Act, 38
Columbia, SC, 15
Columbus, NM, 43
Committee on Public Information, 53
Congressional Government: A Study in American Politics, 19
Cox, James M., 62
Creel, George, 53

D

Davidson College, 15
Democratic Party, 9, 29, 30, 31, 40, 47, 56, 62
"dollar diplomacy," 42

E

"eating clubs," 24, 25
electoral vote, 31, 47
Employers' Liability Commission, 28
Espionage Act, 53

F

Federal Farm Loan Act, 36
Federal Reserve Act, 36
Federal Reserve notes, 36
Federal Reserve System, 36
Federal Trade Commission Act, 38
Fourteen Points address, 7–8, 55, 57

G

Grayson, Colonel Cary, 34

H

Harding, Warren G., 62, 64
Hay-Pauncefote Treaty, 41
Hughes, Charles Evans, 47

I

income tax, 36

J

Johns Hopkins University, 19

L

League of Nations, 8, 9, 16, 58–59, 61, 62, 64, 65–67
Lightfoots, the, 16
Lodge, Henry Cabot, 58–59
Lusitania, 43, 44

M

McAdoo, William Gibbs, 33

N

National Association for the Advancement of Colored People (NAACP), 40
"New Freedom," 31, 34, 35
"New Nationalism," 31
Nineteenth Amendment, 51
1920 presidential election, 62
Nobel Prize for Peace, 65–67

P

Panama tolls, 41
Paris Peace Conference, 8, 56–57
popular vote, 31
preceptors, 24–25
Princeton University (College of New Jersey), 10, 16, 17, 20, 21, 24–27, 29, 30

Wilson's controversial
    legacy at, 26–27
Woodrow Wilson
    School of Public and
    International Affairs,
    26
Progressive Party, 31

R

Renick and Wilson, 17
Republican Party, 8, 9, 31,
    40, 41, 47, 56, 59, 62, 67
Roosevelt, Theodore, 31, 35

S

Sayre, Francis B., 33
segregation, 26, 27, 40
Selective Service Act, 53
"self-determination"
    speech, 56
Sherman Antitrust Act, 38
Sixteenth Amendment, 36
Staunton, VA, 12

T

Taft, William Howard, 31, 32

U

Underwood-Simmons
    Tariff Act, 35

United Nations, 10, 37
US Congress, 7, 34, 35, 36,
    41, 49, 56
US House of
    Representatives, 51
US Senate, 7, 9, 51, 58, 59

V

Veracruz, Mexico, 42
Versailles, Treaty of, 8, 9,
    57–59
Villa, Pancho, 43
Virginia, University of, 17

W

Wesleyan University, 21
Wilson, Edith, 34, 59, 61, 63
Wilson, Eleanor, 22, 32, 33
Wilson, Ellen, 22, 33–34
Wilson, James, 12
Wilson, Jessie, 22, 33
Wilson, Joseph Ruggles, 12
Wilson, Woodrow
    birth and childhood,
        12–15
    in college, 15–19
    as a college professor,
        20–22
    effect of Civil War on,
        13–14
    election to the presi-
        dency, 31

family, 11, 12
foreign affairs, 41–46
health issues, 16, 22, 57, 59
as a lawyer, 17–19
life in the White House, 32–34
marriage and family life, 22–24
as New Jersey governor, 28, 29–30
as Princeton University president, 24–27
publications, 21–22
racial views, 40–41
reforms as president, 34–38
struggle for international peace, 7–8, 55–57
support for women's suffrage, 51
women's suffrage, 51
Woodrow, Janet (Jessie), 12
Woodrow, Thomas, 12
Woodrow Wilson House, 61
Workers' Compensation Act, 28

World War I, 43–46, 51, 61, 67
  American mobilization for, 49–53
  America's role in, 53–55
World War II, 9, 67

Z

Zimmermann Telegram, 49